The

Interrogation

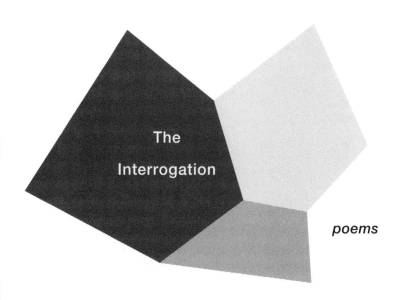

The
Interrogation

poems

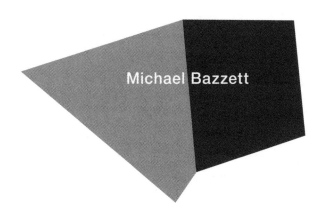

Michael Bazzett

MILKWEED EDITIONS

Published 2017 by Milkweed Editions
Printed in the United States of America
Cover design by Mary Austin Speaker
Cover photograph © Alec Soth/Magnum Photos
Author photo by Leslie Bazzett
17 18 19 20 21 5 4 3 2 1
First Edition

Milkweed Editions, an independent nonprofit publisher, gratefully acknowledges sustaining support from the Jerome Foundation; the Lindquist & Vennum Foundation; the McKnight Foundation; the National Endowment for the Arts; the Target Foundation; and other generous contributions from foundations, corporations, and individuals. Also, this activity is made possible by the voters of Minnesota through a Minnesota State Arts Board Operating Support grant, thanks to a legislative appropriation from the arts and cultural heritage fund, and a grant from Wells Fargo. For a full listing of Milkweed Editions supporters, please visit milkweed.org.

Library of Congress Cataloging-in-Publication Data

Names: Bazzett, Michael, author.
Title: The interrogation : poems / Michael Bazzett.
Description: Minneapolis : Milkweed Editions, 2017.
Identifiers: LCCN 2017019915 (print) | LCCN 2017020020 (ebook) | ISBN 9781571319623 (ebook) | ISBN 9781571314932 (pbk. : alk. paper)
Classification: LCC PS3602.A999 (ebook) | LCC PS3602.A999 A6 2017 (print) | DDC 811/.6--dc23
LC record available at https://lccn.loc.gov/2017019915

Milkweed Editions is committed to ecological stewardship. We strive to align our book production practices with this principle, and to reduce the impact of our operations in the environment. We are a member of the Green Press Initiative, a nonprofit coalition of publishers, manufacturers, and authors working to protect the world's endangered forests and conserve natural resources. *The Interrogation* was printed on acid-free 30% postconsumer-waste paper by Versa Press.

for Leslie

Contents

The

Interrogation

Cruelty

Then you walk into a sodden field.

It is early and smells of rain and pine.
You sense sun beyond the thin clouds.
The earth mushes beneath each footfall
and buried twigs snap beneath your soles.

Soon you are standing before a fence
made of two strands of rusted wire.
Tufts of hair are caught on its barbs,
lifting in the wind like animals.

Beyond the fence is a blank fog.
You cannot quite make out those
gathered in the whiteness beyond.
You hear only the clink of cutlery
and a child crying. There will

be no gunfire, no serrated light.

The cold will be enough, as always.

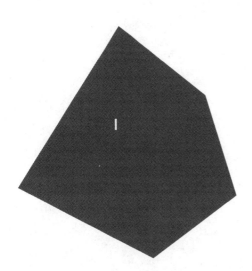

The City

Once we were ten miles outside the city, it
vanished completely. We suspected this
happened from the top down, with television
antennae fading into ether and asphalt
shingles glimmering, like fish scales,
then flecking into nothingness.
                                For a mere
moment buildings were reduced to rib cage,
people illuminated within the lattice of beams,
bent over ironing boards and countertops,
chopping cucumbers into slender green coins
until they and their knives and even the blade-
scarred board had vanished into empty air.

But there were also those who asserted
buildings softened into something like
sodden cardboard and settled slowly into
themselves. One contingent even claimed
nothing happened at all: the city simply
shifted like a sleeping animal, dreaming
of our return.
                        We decided to confirm
our top-down theory by hiding a camera
in the woven branches of a linden tree
then climbing into our van and driving
until the city sank into the dusky horizon.

There, someone said, pointing, *it's done it again.*

And it was true, the impassive brick and steel
were gone. We cranked a U-turn and rumbled
home over the asphalt we'd just traveled
in hopes of catching our city in the breathless
unclothed moment before she had once again
reassembled herself, down to bits of rusted
hardware on the roadside and the actors
hired to loiter outside of bars.
      But this time,
as we coasted slowly into our neighborhood,
past the impostors and hastily reconstructed
but nonetheless convincing details, we smiled
quietly at one another.

      The van creaked to a stop under the tree
and we leaned the ladder into its thick crown

when suddenly something lifted
scraping into flight, croaking
like a rusted door—

as if the tree had cracked
open and coughed its dark
and broken
heart into the sky—

At Night

after Simic

at night you might not sense
the old hatreds of the city
which could be anywhere
rain-swept pavement turns
to shining lakes of light
or cars hiss coldly through
brushstroked intersections

the people are stacked away
into vertical burrows filled
with pill bottles and screens
insomniacs lie awake and share
the blank stare of their many
separate ceilings and children
are taught to shoot the dead-
bolt upon first returning home

and yet the city wakes each day
and puts on its face and nods
as if it is not a family gathered
around the scrape of cutlery
at a steaming evening meal
pretending grandma never
used scissors on the mailman
and that father did not slip
his hands into his niece's
blouse just this afternoon

Nowhere

Nothing will happen tonight
on an unknown rain-darkened street
at the door of the Hotel Nowhere.

When the cathedral bells fall silent
you will know it is the moment.

The password is any form of the verb
to be. The ritual will be enacted
by the most reverend Pastor Niemand

and will be attended by those that matter
less and less with each passing day.

You will know you are expected
once you conclusively determine
you have received no invitation.

At Half-Island

At Half-Island, slate-gray water breaks
over rock and plasters
  weeds like hair against the granite

It has been this way for years

   the sea always swelling

   the tides in flux

   the breathing of the world

And anyone who pauses to sit
and watch the sea do its work

will feel a deep-breathing swell
  slowly fill
      the channels of their body

            *

When the tide left the orca
slack on the rock

the men went out in tall oyster-boots
to take its teeth

They had a fine-gauge blade
for the enamel

Each tooth worn and grooved
as wood

a single one would fill your palm
with its heft

like an old flint-knife
found in a cave

*

One look at the angled whale

said something
was lodged in its belly

and soon the men
were cursing and gawping

as they pulled
the better part
of a moose out

including one
fine-hoofed foreleg
folded neat
as a camp chair
and half a rack
of splintered antler

*

I could see it then:

The wild-eyed moose
  jolted in its crossing
   as the water
swelled fat and black
 around his churning
then dragged quickly down
   to be bolted
in torn hunks
  where the broken
antler did its piercing work
     and the orca's dark
life drained slowly
    into its own belly

    *

Maybe it is already
  too late to talk
  about appetite

or how we live
with rock and water
yet listen to neither

or how we cannot recognize
  ourselves when delivered
to ourselves through signs

as when our souls
    take the form of gulls

    crying again and again
the one
    sharp word

    we all have in common—

The Central Registry

I slip two nights between the wooden slats.

We store them upright
to discourage warping.
Because night has a memory.

They are wrapped in brown paper,
tied up snug with twine
and surprisingly flat once folded.

I label each one neatly with a permanent marker
affixing a label to the spine for that very purpose

and then move on
to the moonlight

which needs to be poured into an aquarium
with a fungicidal solution.

So much moonlight is sickly these days.

Once, the twine broke
on a night long ago
and it started coming on—

the paper burst
with the snap of a small bore rifle

and it unfurled
like a black wing.

The force of it split the pine of the storage rack
and filled the warehouse with a pitchy blackness.

It was a fine specimen, midwinter,
late nineteenth century, moonless,
cold as a brass bell and utterly still.

You don't see many nights
like that anymore.

Not that I'm nostalgic.

This job brooks no sentiment.
Not once you've smelled moonlight
when it's gone round the bend.

Ithaca

I had that slight burst one gets with the third glass
of wine and decided to walk to sunny Ithaca, white
rock like a tooth through blue water. No stallion land,
but good for goats. Or so I'm told. I excused myself
from the olives & brie and slipped out the side door.

The green of my back lawn at dusk was luminous.
The sounds of the party sifted through the screen
fading to bird-chatter as I began to cross the fields,
my good shoes made sodden in a matter of minutes.
When I reached the shore in the middle of the night,

wet pebbles grated with each soft step and I could
hear the rasping footfalls of perhaps a dozen others,
their dark shapes mingling with the hulking granite.
There was no moon, barely enough light to catch
the glint of a blade raised at the end of one arm.

Who is it? hissed a frightened voice. Who are *you*?
I asked. And my voice cracked like a broken clarinet.
I heard pebbles shift, and then one shadow started
to laugh. You sound like you're twelve, he chuckled.
Let him go, he said to the others, and before they

could change their minds I leapt over the collapsing
white lip of that first wave and was running like a boy
across the tremulous roof of the sea.

They Held It in Their Hands

The torso of the machine was burlap stuffed with feathers,
with limbs made of old cutlery, and every time it scratched
itself or placed one pious hand upon its heart, a downy cloud
erupted from its bowels like barely stifled laughter. Soon

it became a shredded mess, and all the children followed
it clanking through the streets to shriek their airplane sounds
and run with arms outstretched through the floating down
as it dragged the body of whomever had been the latest

to say something wrong. It used pushpins to tack the body
to a post so we could finger paint our messages in the clouds
using only the warmest blood. This became our congress
on those warm afternoons, and we grew more and more

grateful to the simple machine for the white-hot sensation
of cleanliness it offered us. Righteous anger is just rage
wearing a velvet tracksuit. I want my anger to be warm
and naked as the day it first opened its eyes to the world.

The Unnerving Thing

Out there the crowd stands
in the cold square
silent as an animal,

bootsoles shifting as they wait.

The unnerving thing
is how their breath
hangs in the air
as a heaving shroud:

you don't expect
our warmth

to be the thing
that obscures us.

The Cellar

The door scraped open with a wet sound.
Their eyes caught the light and the cold
fluorescence fluttered as they disappeared
into cracks that seemed too small to hold
rats. It might have been a battered pile
of shoes sprung to life yet there was one
twitchy hulk that did not disappear. She
huddled in the corner to nurse her babes.
I went over to see them, naked as thumbs,
and everyone shrieked, Get the fuck away!
You'll lose a fingertip. But I heard nothing
as I knelt to watch the near translucence
of those bodies pulse and shine with life.

Everybody

was held inside
the warm folds
of the weave

clucking and drunk
on the smell of milk

fat tit loosened
from slack-lipped
breathing

and when asked
if they belonged
to the greatest

nation in the world
they nuzzled the tit

then bared
their tiny fangs
and nipped

and the milk
ran pink

and tasted
of iron

Sunflowers

In August, when goldfinches
come to land on the bristled faces

come to lock into that curved
sponginess with the hooked

nails of their feet come to beak
into the polleny disks and pluck

the seed casks come to crack
and shred the husks come to stab

the oily meal the sunflowers
nod yes heavily like a clutch

of old women bobbing repeatedly
yes from their benches in the shade

goading the hesitant child—
it's okay, you should try it, it's good.

The Subterranean Room

is small

      and smells faintly
of wine and metal

and we have been inside it

ever since light split the sky like the skin

of an overripe fruit

and we understood
      there was no way

the sound rumbling up through our soles

 (as we stood outside
  staring at the luminous fractures)

could portend anything good

and so we hid
      in this place

our father made
  and stocked with provisions

     and we waited

until the sound
      of vaguely human voices

drew us to the surface
            like sirens—

Okay

Let's kill everyone, they said. Okay, said the boy.

Let's make it clean, they said. Like the outside
of an egg. Okay, said the boy. We'll give you
the haircut now. And this neckerchief. Here's
the salute. Okay, said the boy. We'll make

the whole enterprise smell of mint and sell it
in embossed tins. Mmmm, said the boy,
I love mint. Yes, they said. Of course you do.

II

The Dawdler

Wake me if you've heard this
poem before

but not yet, not quite.
Let me slip into the dream

beneath these lines, cool
as the other side

of the pillow. I like the one
about Chuang Tzu especially,

dreaming he was a butterfly
dreaming he was a man

like two mirrors
hung on opposite walls

facing one another
in endless hunger.

The Interrogation

There is no two-way mirror. No bare bulb suspended on a wire
above a metal table. I simply watch him from the kitchenette
as he stares out the window at a parking lot. The passing trucks
shake the grass on the median into patterns. The window unit
spits onto the asphalt. The coming day will be quite hot.

A plastic cup of water rests before him. Later I'll shut off the AC
and dangle the possibility of a swim. He's always loved the feeling
of submersion. That sudden hush of slipping underwater to buoy
free from the pull of earth. He hasn't shaved for three days.

It's strange to see his beard come in so dark. My whiskers have
gone silver these past years. He is lean and brown from the sun,
despite this time indoors, and I admire the easy musculature as it
shifts beneath his skin. His children are young, one not yet born.
He does not know why he is here but is tiring of the questions.

After a pause, we begin again. I walk over to the table and sit,
recognizing the wary lift of his eyebrows when I say, Why not
just tell me who you are? And once again he mutters my name.

I was, of course, initially surprised he did not recognize me. Then
annoyed. Yet in the end it is liberating to watch him stare past
my eyes like window glass, trying to make out the details of what
lies inside. There are things about him I don't recognize as well.
He is less talkative than anticipated, more inscrutable. His quiet
anger often comes across as confidence. Though I know better,

the effect is striking and I find myself giving him more credit than he deserves. When I agreed to this, I thought the condition of only asking questions was clever. I didn't realize how much pressure it would place on me. I keep thinking of the old song: *Life is a joke that's just begun.* But I'm on the other end of it now and I hear the words as *Life is a joke best left unspoken.*

In the Himalayas

I.

I climbed the mountain
to where the old man sat
nested in his white beard.

Look to the moon, he said,
and learn that you will be
shaved down to nothing;

you will be skinned clean;
you will be eaten by sky
and become only darkness.

Okay, I said. Point taken.

That was when I noticed
he was levitating
about an inch above the granite.

Can you go any higher?
I asked.

Not really, he said,
but I can do this—

And he gave a gentle push
using only his fingertips

and coasted over the rock
like butter in a warm pan.

Would you like to try it?

I nodded and reached out
and gave him a firm nudge
as I would a plastic puck

riding its cushion of air
on an air hockey table
in a suburban basement

only realizing my error
once his bewildered face
glided over

the edge of the cliff.

II.

The next guy looked
pretty much like the first:
turban, lotus position, etc.

He started speaking
as soon as I arrived:

The moon instructs us
how to be whittled

down, sliver by sliver,
like a shard of bone—

Got it, I nodded.

He looked at me kind of
quizzical and suspicious.

And maybe a little
disappointed, like
he was just getting warmed up.

He opened his mouth
to offer a bit more
but I held up my hand:

Seriously, man. Duly noted.
The first guy filled me in—

His eyes lit with delight.
You know Kevin?

I smiled and nodded,
like I was chuckling at
what a rascal Kevin was:

Dude lives on the edge.
Know what I'm saying?

It's the Himalayas, man,
he said, his smile vanishing.
We all live on the edge.

III.

The jails in the Himalayas
are not nearly as cold
as one might expect.

They are also unexpectedly
generous with the yak butter
and the secondhand tea.

So much of life is about
managing expectations,
I thought. I reached

to scratch my head,
forgetting for a moment
the bamboo slivers

beneath my fingernails
and the iron cuff
that held my wrist

chained to the wall
where I leaned
in the chilled alpine light.

The Earth Inside

I dug into the earth
inside me and felt it
thicken under my nails
as I clawed damp dirt.

I packed it in one hand
until the clod was dense
and wanted to be held
as a gun-grip or grenade

and then thrust it out
and said, Look at this,
the darkness of my heart.

No one there to laugh
or even wince, and I felt
chagrined at this impulse
to mock the discovery
of such fertility inside.

The Silence

the silence
of the tree

before the fire
cracks it

open with its
tooth of heat

and blade
of light

is the silence
I hear now

in this rain-
softened wood

where each
limb is slick

with wet
and the trees

have shed
their suits

to vein
the sky—

The Man with No Mouth

I can't tell you how happy I am to announce
how happy I am. No, really. I can't tell you—

I have no mouth, only the skin of my chin
curving up into the twin caverns of a mundane

nose with an uninterrupted blankness beneath.
It is a form of erasure, I'd say, if I could say

anything. Your sense of smell must be quite keen,
said the man on the bus as I stared pointedly away.

It's not for him to say what's blessing, what's curse.
But the truth is I can keep a secret like a stone.

The Matrons

The matrons walk into the ballroom.
Tastefully dressed and strung

in pearls
they quietly surround me:

the line they murmur
is always the same:
Do you want to dance upstairs,

from behind?
You can have all of us. It will be

like a forest.
And how much does the house
take? I ask.

Thirty-three and a third.
And what do the trees
say?

The elms whisper

rainfall and the pines
needle one another

but the broken
oak with its yellow heart

opened by the storm
says nothing:
we love to listen to it

stab at the truth.

There Are Things We Cannot See

for Tran Dan

Over time

the nipple
is shaped

by the mouth
of the child

*

the sun spreads
the hips and legs
of tender grass

to enter it
to the root

*

there is flesh
and hunger

everywhere
in the world

*

we grow one
into the other

*

there is
the desire
to clothe

and the desire
to become
unbound

*

put a naked
man in a crowd

and watch us

make a human
palisade
around him

*

drag your hand
through the air

and it leaves
no trail—

spear the lake
it leaves no mark

*

yet here is
the whorled

cave of your navel

where a thin river
once coursed

*

and your nose
still flared
by breathing

*

and your eyes
wet wounds

where light
comes in

*

your face
the scar

of what
we all
must

remember

Moles

In the dirt beneath the mattress
where I sleep here in the forest
there is the purest deepest
blackness and the moles

are slow comets
with tiny pink hands—

My Body Is Not an Axe

I fill a box with silence and bring it
to you to open and you look at me
and say nothing then you shake your head

and say No, this too is a poem—
I want something that tells the truth
without a box without figure without

metaphor and so I return to my workshop
to set it ablaze and after days of smoldering
I bathe in the still-warm ashes and come

running for you to see the raised welts
and my ashen skin and you say I'm afraid
this is mere performance so I run

to the shore out past the heaved and broken
ice where I crash into the water mouth
open to let it fill me and rinse me clean—

Nobody Fails at Meditation

Nobody fails at meditation
like I do.

They say,
Note the arrival of thoughts

and allow them to pass through
like clouds crossing a summer sky.

Let judgment go.

But one cloud
is always running

like a woman with a torn dress

with the wind pressing its folds
against her body

and I suddenly wish
to wheel around on my horse

and thunder back to the farmhouse,
spattering her white frock

with mud as I swing from the saddle
into her trembling arms.

On the One Hand

On the one hand: What I see happen
is more important than what happened
because there is no what happened

separate from what I see. On the other:
The brick hit my head. I did not see it

hit my head. I am nonetheless

dead. Language is not
human invention

but an extension
of evolution

flowing from the throat.

Thoughts rise
like antlers.

To the Woman Drinking Three Gin & Tonics
with Her Breakfast Enchiladas

I broke my rule
about beginning poems with ballpoint pens
in sturdy lines on legal pads
before making the potentially premature transition
to Garamond

because I simply could not wait
to speak of your floppy hat,
your black print dress and espadrilles
and your comfortably sagging
posture that somehow announced, *I could give*

zero fucks about your opinions on morning gin—
in a tone that was not only ingratiating
but zen, without the merest whiff of dissolution
given the care with which you perused the Op-Ed section of the
    newspaper.

I could say that I wished you were my mother
but that would be both sentimental and inaccurate
given that the love I felt
when you nonchalantly ordered your third gin
was as fierce and sad as a wounded animal.

Now, this was not an image
I planned on including here; it just sort of arrived
in a turn that somehow meshed with my internal sense of logic
even if it did cause me to wonder

if it might have been crossed out back on that legal pad
had I taken the time to actually draft this—

No, the love I felt was as complicated
as the dreams you must have had
once you'd finished your enchiladas and wandered
home to an empty apartment that you filled to the brim
with the sonorous waves of your sleep.

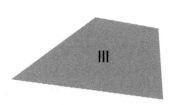

The Phone Call

The phone rang
in the darkness.
The quiet voice
was breathless:

I brought you
into this world
of endless pain

and I can take
you out again.

Hi Mom, I said.

It was quiet
for a moment.

How could you
tell it was me,
she replied.

I just let the
silence hang,
very suave-like.

Well, anyway,
she sighed,
Happy Birthday.

Lazarus

after Elizabeth Jennings

When Lazarus walked from the grave,
he tottered like a child letting go of a table
heading into the open for the first time.

His muscles were weak. Due to being dead,
I suppose. He was pale and waxy as a grub,
another drained thing out of the heavy

darkness. The smell confirmed it. Scent
cannot lie, it seems, and though this had
been the object of his mother's prayers,

when she hugged him and let the focus
of his eyes settle upon her like melting ice,
there was no doubt that part of what her

convoluted expression was grappling with
was the smell of meat gone round the bend.
Later, when he had bathed and dressed

in a clean robe she thought she'd folded
for the last time, she could still smell it,
a slight rank sweetness, like an orchid

in its final days, feeding its bloom with
one white toe in the dark earth. Only
this was decay delayed. This was birth.

The Birth

He was born wearing a worsted-wool suit and emerged
with his hair slightly mussed, his hand extended toward
the attending physician to congratulate him on the delivery.

Those wing tips must have hurt, murmured the doctor,
noting the uncanny shine on the tiny shoes. The boy spat
out the tit five minutes later and insisted upon bottled milk,

warmed on the stovetop with a touch of brandy. Yes sir,
said his mother deferentially, not pausing to consider
the place from whence the little man had come.

When He Was a Boy

an angel handed him an envelope
with the day of his death
etched in letterpress
on beautiful handmade paper

but not the year

and every year since
as dusk falls
on the anniversary

the boy climbs into a hole
dug into his yard

and asks his loved ones
to rain shovelfuls of dirt
upon his body

He lies on his side
with his knees drawn
to his chest

and his arms folded
into the warm curl
of his body

his eyes closing
as the dark clumps
leap about him

and he feels
the gathering weight
begin to hold him

In his teenage years
in a fit of metaphor
he insisted

that the garden hose
be drawn into the hole
so that the fetus
might have its cord

and the next year
he fashioned a red felt cloak
to wear over his Sunday best

Now that he has lived
for seven decades
this has become

the occasion for something
resembling a party
his children
drink champagne

and his grandchildren
hold his hands
as the boy gingerly descends

the wooden steps
he built so long ago
for this very purpose

The Fable of the Man

He threw his coat from the bridge.
It hit the water with a *whuff*

and hung there for a moment
before it absorbed its surroundings

and slipped beneath the surface
suddenly intent on the bottom of things.

That was my skin, cried the man.
Now I'm a mollusk shed of its shell.

Calm down, said his mother,
for the man was only three years old.

Youth is one of those infections
from which most everyone recovers.

Early November

The man stood on a table in the town square.
Its base was cement and the tabletop was etched
with the outline of a chessboard but no one had
played the game there for years, if ever. The grid

served as ghost for the faint hopes of the town
planner or parks department employee who had
briefly envisioned kindly old men playing chess—
or even checkers—in the park beneath a tree. But

no tree. Just hot sun and cold wind and poured
concrete benches too close to the base of the table
for a grown pair of knees. The man used the bench
as a step then placed both feet square on the table

and stood there, arms hanging at his sides, eyes
fixed on the dried and battered grass, stark naked.
There was nothing comic about this, nothing
performative. He just stood there, hands cupped

over his privates, with no sign and no explanation,
but we could read the lines that gravity had written
on his body with its downward-pulling pen, the fine
skin that wrinkled like tissue paper in every joint,

how his under-color grew slate grey after hours
in the cold. Why are you doing this? someone
finally asked. A small knot of us had gathered—
dog walkers, exercisers—and now the morning

sun disappeared and the day began to smell
of rain. He did not answer. We could see blue
veins mapping his breast fat and a small raised
scar purpled like a lilac on his lower abdomen.

When the rain began, we remained out there.
He shivered visibly as the cold rivulets tracked
the contours of his body, as his thin hair plastered
his skull like wet grass, and our eyes could trace

their fingertips over the braille of his gooseflesh.
That was when we realized that he was never
coming down, that he would topple like a pillar
and be carried away, limbs angled like firewood,

his body finally finished with what it had to say.
One woman approached him then and said, Please.
Won't you please come down? The words seemed
unnaturally loud, as if she had had to shout over

the rising applause of the rain. He said nothing.
His gaze remained fixed on nothing. He offered
us nothing as he shook and chattered with the cold
and we stood in silence and waited for him to fall.

Country Squire Landscape Services

It looks like a storm's threatening to break, said Rollie.

I was picking moist clumps of grass from under the mower
hoods. We'd just loaded them onto the trailer and were debating
whether or not to hustle to the next job, or maybe pause and
roll a joint.

Well, let it break then, I said. I'm calling its bluff.

It wasn't bluffing. The sky split clean open, like the peel on
an overripe plum, and an inky blackness showed through the
wound. It was blacker than black and moved like a muscle. And
then we felt the suction and our hair was flowing forward and
we watched a huge cloud of starlings get inhaled into the void.

More and more birds were drawn into the blackness, through
the place where the sky had torn. And then things began to
fly that weren't alive, like fast-food wrappers and leaves shorn
from the treetops. Even the damp grass clippings began to stir.
A loose strand of crows lifted skyward. Then a great blue heron
went wheeling, its legs trailing like roots. And it too was gone.

Fucking A, man, said Rollie, who pretty much always said that,
no matter what.

A less spiritual man might have been worried. But somehow
I knew that in another world, two men stood in an open field.
They were tall and strong and beautiful and they were pointing
to the sky, where bird after bird came spinning down like rain.

IV

Confessions

There is a sound you make when you exhale
through your nose that contains nine octaves.
Your fingers are small animals that burrow
into me and sleep guileless as children.

Your tongue once visited me on its own.
It arrived with a train case and a list
of demands incongruous with the posture
of the fat pink comma on my doorstep.

Pound for pound, I'm the strongest
muscle in your body, it announced.
But it could not gain any leverage when
I flicked it from the stoop with a broom.

Once I reached my opened hand
into your chest and was startled
to find another hand waiting there.
It was the first handshake of my life
that did not feel contrived.

Island

I remember haunted half-pained foolish
laughter breaking loose of him on the island
the coal barge rumbling by sweeping our tent
with a cold and shocking light that drove him
out into the wet sand where he stood a raving
antic figure half-enjoying how utterly fucked

up he still was on the pills weed whatever
else might feed a hungry seventeen years
harrying a cornfield town where dogs fell
asleep behind the church—when the call
came this morning thirty years onward
I already knew what and only wondered

how?

and why now?

Other Names for Fire

for Mark Leidner

1. Kiss-me-not.
2. He who grows hungrier the more he's fed.
3. Sunlight released from the prison of the tree.
4. Rust on meth.
5. Creature made of tongue and wing.
6. Naughty flower.
7. Soul of the coal.
8. A single neuron sizzling in the mind of the Sun.
9. A chandelier of lickings.
10. Idiot's lip gloss.
11. Bourbon of the Air.
12. Lucifer's bouquet.
13. The cave dancer's doppelgänger.
14. The glint in the eye of the gun.
15. Yellow hat, orange shirt, red pants, blue shoes.

The Fact

that you are you and I am I
is no less stunning for being commonplace.

The bronchial architecture of our breath
holds the memory of trees.

All creation funnels into and through our bodies.
This is true of everyone
who encounters these words. Except

for the one of you
who happens to be the aberrant replication.
And what is unnerving

is that even as you read these words
you are still convinced you are human.

This was the clever twist
they infused into the new consciousness
to echo the old consciousness

and why the sadness you sometimes feel
is hard to locate, why you read
poems in the first place,

looking again and again
for what cannot possibly be there.

The Mechanic

1.

The mechanic closed the hood
and sidled over to us, wiping
his hands on an oily rag.
He offered a mirthless smile
then said, I'm afraid

the tumor's grown. The solenoid
is compromised. It's going to be
touch and go, a delicate procedure—

And as he spoke you took my hand
and whispered something—

And I thought of that winter morning
when you'd unwrapped the little box
and held that shiny red body in your hand
rolling it over the couch cushions,
the tiny chrome wheels churning
as you purred engine sounds
in the back of your throat.

2.

The mechanic closed the hood
and sidled over to us, wiping
his hands on an oily rag.

He offered a mirthless smile
then said, I'm afraid

there's nothing I can do.
I never actually trained
for this. My focus was
haphazard. I wanted only
to be a dancer.

3.

The mechanic closed the hood
and sidled over to us, wiping
his hands on an oily rag.
He offered a mirthless smile
then said, There is no quiet

like winter quiet. The bronchial
architecture of the forest laid bare—

That's beautiful, you said.

Would you mind if we took it
and slipped it under the hood
to see if we could get this thing going?

4.

The mechanic closed the hood
and sidled over to us, wiping
his hands on an oily rag.

He offered a mirthless smile
then said, I'm afraid

That's all he said. I'm afraid

So you took my hand
and we ran into the night.

The Encounter

Sometimes I wake before my eyes do

And my face is smeared across the mirror

That is what his face looked like, the man
who half-fell from the darkened doorway
like a shadow separating from its darkness

He grabbed my wrist and pulled me face-to-face

His stale breath held the memory of coffee
and the fermented scent of a slow river

When I tried to jerk free I felt the bony
bracelet of his fingers lock into itself

He meant only to hold me close and speak
whatever wild words he needed to say

His eyes caught the gloss of the streetlights

But his words came out as animal sounds
or the idiot-slur of a man who's gussed the bed
and he soon melted into whimpering moans

I pulled my wrist out quick and ran
thudding through the night

another heavy-footed boy struck
dumb by the man I had become

Gag

The words catch in the throat
a clotted sound as the gun
barrel clicks against the back

teeth. This must be some sort
of gag, you think reflexively, not
certain what to do with the sound

of metal on enamel in a scene
that hinges on the phrase
This is just a gag, just a reflex

action taken by the hands and the
arms themselves while your tired
mind settles into a chair to watch.

Rain

A horse is made of meat and bone.
Yet mine is made of mud and grass.
I built it up with slapping hands
when rain came over the mountains.

Then slowly I worked its thick
form free with a sodden sound
and galloped the rain-soft ground
as sun broke the clouds wide open.

The wind was cold and earth-scent
flared my nostrils with each step.
There is no bit or saddle. We fit

like folded hands. I pass wavering
stands of birch and then villages
where the women lift their heads
while cutting carrots on a board.

I ride for days and then rain
returns. The horse grows
so heavy its hooves begin
to split on stones and I know

that it will soon return
into the earth like a lover.

Last Exit

There was only the one rabbit, quivering softly.
The heather of its pelt made me want to run
my hand through the grain, its jaw working
clover into paste. And chickens. Some looked
sick, beaks curved and cracked like broken nails.
Others were wired to strut and peck, cleansing
the field of insects. Eggs lay like stones among
the tufts, cracked and weeping fluid, and steers
stood idly, switching tails at flies as puckered
backsides shat sauce like faucets. Ducks tucked
their greasy heads beneath their wings, curled
in feathered ovals by the stillness of the pond
filled with oil. The field was rimmed with thyme
and stands of fat-eared corn, tumbling stacks
of melons, zucchinis, tomatoes softening to rot.
A hillock of potatoes, purple, brown, whiskered,
leached a fermented trickle toward the fishy mass,
heaped with mussels, skinned and gutted albacore,
and the crumpled filamented bodies of shrimp
lumped into a pile. Everywhere the pungent
smell of waste. The word *fecund* comes to mind,
I said to the man standing beside me, the words
slightly muffled by my sanitary mask. It's just you,
he shrugged. You don't smell it too? I asked.
He shook his head. No, it's just *you*. All of this
passed through the turnings of your body. It is
you. I arched my eyebrows in a way that normally
conveys just the right tone of appreciative wonder,
but it failed to have the desired effect and I stood

chastened among the noise and thickening smells.
Boars snuffled the mounds heaped across the field,
and I felt I should say something clever about how
you are what you eat, but I dithered and the man
walked out to a faraway shed, where a light flicked
on and a generator shuddered to life and I heard
the whine of the blade as the pigs began to squeal.

The Telepathic Heart

exists in a book.
    I will not say exists
        only in a book
as I do not know if the telepathic heart as a species
possesses other natural habitats. But this telepathic
heart lived in a book that was also a chest
   which is a fitting locale for a heart but was
perhaps not the sort of chest you envision
     as it was more like a cigar box
or a tiny sea chest.
     Its pages had been hollowed out
to form a box with a brass clasp on a leather strap
that could hide cigarettes, cyanide, or microfilm,
while its aged spine stared placidly from the shelf
and Stasi agents tore the room to shreds
  driving switchblades into pillows
    to fill the air with clouds of swirling down.

We know the heart was telepathic
    because it named its love
without once encountering its beloved
    then seized & flexed like a fat porpoise
and soon expired in its gilt-edged hollow
which was perhaps a bit too airless and small.
It did not offer this information under any duress.
There was no table under a bare bulb. It simply
exhaled the name of its soul mate
    and that was that. I wish we could say
no animals were harmed in the making of this poem

but that porpoise is dead as a cutlet
                    as is the telepathic heart
which is too bad, as we would have liked to ask it
a few questions about the curious and hidden nature
                    of what we often refer to as love.

For the Person I Have Not Met

There's no other way to put it: I love you

in the way someone loves the silk lining
her pocket: without a thought and not
at all. After all, why should I? You're not
me. Given these arrangements, I know
it is unlikely you can hear the thunder
humming the timbers of this darkened
house. The clouds, chiseled white this
morning, have now begun to dissolve
in hairy curtains of rain, lashing trees.

Trust is not a word you offer the sky.
As soon as you look, a cloud changes
its mind. Whim. Flux. Loose change
on the wet floor of a bar and you
too lazy to pick up the coins I left
so that you could pay attention.

On the Subway

When I detach them and slip them into your shopping bag,
you do not complain. Mostly because you do not notice.

I maintain my signature eye contact—part menace, part
charm—and let one hand glide to my fly where I'm now
so good at undoing the series of springs and tiny hooks
it takes little more effort than coughing. The clandestine
drop is the perilous part. One waits for a lurch as the car
curves into a bend so the weighted bag sways sideways
and the added heft is lost in that gentle pendulous force.

Performance art is on its way out, they say. But just wait
until you arrive home and find the quiet coil of my privates
at the bottom of your Tiffany's bag, with a hand-lettered
card explaining that art means putting yourself out there
even if all you have to offer is a handful of inscrutable junk.

Miles

If somebody told me I only had one hour to live,
I'd spend it choking a white man. —MILES DAVIS

He said he'd do it nice and slow,
trumpeter fingers clamping valves
to regulate airflow and bend that
final note as it left my throat.

I had seen the flyer on the cork
bulletin board asking for volunteers
interested in meeting Miles Davis.

You'll have Miles to go
before you sleep, it quipped—
a joke so pale it had to be
penned by a white man.

The rendezvous was set at eight
and I wore my secondhand
jacket with the western yoke.

They gave me a paper cup
filled with weak coffee.

Miles arrived almost an hour late
and said, *We gonna do this or what?*

I smiled, which was assent enough
and as he walked toward me
I sensed the coming embrace.

I Went to the Market

I went to the market to sell this
body because the man said take

what is living and make it dead
capital and build a pile of coins.

Okay, I said and I climbed onto
my bike and pedaled downtown

where I found a spot in the sun
and disrobed and felt the warm

light over new parts of my body
and breeze tussling my fine hairs

and I peeled the fresh dressing
from my new tattoo that said

FOR SALE in clean sans-serif font
etched neatly across my heart.

Is this some sort of street theater?
asked an old woman, smiling.

You know, a performance, or
some kind of art installation?

I noticed you placed the tattoo
right where the logo goes. Yes,

I said. So she began to explain
to the gathering crowd what was

happening and put a shoebox
at my feet which slowly filled

with coins. I love how utterly
you ironize the silver, she said.

Right, I said, lifting the heavy
box as I began to follow her

to her car. The sun had sunk
and my junk was getting cold.

What are you doing? she asked.
What are *you* doing? I repeated,

jingling the heavy box to make
my point: I clearly belong to you

now. She stopped and stared
for a long time and finally said,

You're an idiot, aren't you?
Yes, I said, but I'm also a man

of my word.

The Book of My Life

Yesterday I got the news:

it turns out I'm a beautiful
woman and the book
of my life is graced
with an overexposed
image of my face: my eyes
mostly iris and mascara

and floating in the glowing
blankness of my forehead
bumptious and unspeakable
words in an elegant font
the title I've been seeking

and for a moment I simply
sway like summer grass
until my winsome beauty
creeps slowly up on me

and I begin to wonder
if these pages hold my
life or the desires of my
salacious editor and I flip
the book to examine the
bar code and see FICTION
in all caps and I am struck

blind before I can flip
back to that floating title
to copy it quickly down
and the dream ends as it
always does with me

clawing for the iron pencil
fastened to the floor of the sea—

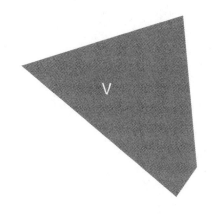

[the words I have not written]

are the ones I follow doggedly into the woods

Perhaps you too will track them through the snow
and we will find ourselves standing in the cold

the smoke of our breath rising as we trade pleasantries
within the scope of their camouflaged eyes—

the fine hairs of your neck will tremble as their hidden
gaze reads your features and you will say, once again,

that what arises from the body is irrefutable

They

They took the world and drained it
white. Paleness was the fashion.
Waistcoats, fingernails, eyelashes
all bleached to a pallid hue: pale
as the rind of the honeydew.
And, of course, there was still
fucking behind closed doors
as there is always a basic amount
of fucking behind closed doors.
The color rises inside a fuck.
That's how you came about.
I mean, I'm sorry to say it here—
but truth is now the fashion
as it adds a certain florid
tinge to the world they
leached of blood to keep
themselves so oddly pale—

The Handshake

I suppose it could wait
until we actually meet,
and extend our hands
one toward the other

in a remnant gesture
extending back to a time
when it served as proof
we'd arrived unarmed.

So it's unlikely I'll stab you.
I'll simply take your hand
and you mine. Neither of us
will try to prove anything

with a crushing grasp. It will
more likely resemble a visit
to the doctor, the same
tenderness and detachment,

searching the small bones
for a possible break. But
what if we don't? Meet,
that is. Is it better that

I wrote this? So you know
you were remembered
before I even knew who
it was I might forget?

The Meat of It

To make a good book you need what William
Faulkner called "the raw meat on the floor."
So before I started in I got some ground beef
and dropped it on the hardwood with a *spat!*
It felt wrong. Like dropping a baby. But I did it
for art. When my son came home from school
he said, Why is there meat on the floor? I said,
Art. He nodded like maybe that made sense
and said, It's kind of freaking me out. I know,
I said, me too. We all have to make sacrifices.
Is that blood leaking out or juice? he asked.
I'm not sure I'm one to make that distinction,
I said, mostly to avoid answering the question.
I didn't tell him how strange it was to unwrap
the meat so carefully, the plastic peeling away
like a onesie on a warm day, and then just sort
of hurl it down at the hardwood with a *spat!*
Are we still going to eat it? he asked after a bit.
I'm not sure, I said. I think it depends upon
a lot of different factors, a lot of ins and outs.
Is this a writing thing? he asked. Because you
have that weird look in your eye. I'm your
father, I said. I held you as a baby. I'd never
use a moment like this just to make a poem.

In the Book

In the book when the boy nearly drowned
his legs tangled in weeds or maybe rope

I was gripped and followed his footsteps
along the dune road to the heavy church
door that eased open at the touch of one hand

breathing cool air out against his face
his sodden trousers wrapping his calves
wet cuffs breaded white with sand

and everyone turned to look and saw
nothing but a dark door haloed with light
pushed opened by a breeze, no boy at all—

the scene was so real that time slipped
into its spiraled shell and pulled its
feelers behind the hinged clasp

and I stood to pour myself a glass
of something strong enough to cut
through the feeling when I opened

those crisp pages again
to find the boy still struggling
to kick himself free

of that grasping kelp
then heave himself
onto the packed sand

his fingers carving
trails as he sputtered
and coughed

and though stunned
was soon fine.

I riffled numbly
forward then back
then forward
again and slowly

searched the entire
book but the scene
at the church was gone.

The Hole

He died and left a hole behind him
in the exact shape of his life.

It took a while for the hole to close,
as if the air had turned to gelatin

and those of us who knew him
noticed how sunlight
now struck the ground
where his shadow once fell

and the wind no longer unfolded
around his wilted posture

and the words of his friends
spun out in threads that did not
catch upon his two-day beard.

Eventually the hole
grew closed without a scar,
just as the current
heals itself behind a man
staggering from a river,

just as his name
slipped our minds—

The Little Things

Once I achieved immortality
I found god took me

for granted. It was evident
in the little things:

the lengthened pauses
in our correspondence,

his increased willingness
to allow me to pay

for the meal even after
he had chosen the wine.

You will have plenty of time
to earn it back, he said.

As usual, he spoke
using only the wind.

The Monster

We didn't notice it at first
because of the adrenaline
coursing through our bodies
but the monster was too old.
Its muzzle had gone grey
and a number of its claws
were cracked and broken.
It even trembled with a bit
of palsy when it settled
back on its fat haunches.
And every time it put
somebody's head into its
mouth and tried to shred it
clean like a plum from a stem
one of its teeth broke and it
howled in pain and spit
the person out with splinters
of brittle enamel clinging
to their sodden clothing
and then they too began
to scream or possibly moan,
if they hadn't already begun
to slip from consciousness.

Strictly half-assed, said Steve
and he dropped the sword
he'd received at the entrance
upon arrival at the warehouse
painted to look like a cave

with a coupon for himself
and five guests to do battle
with a bona fide monster
of "cannibalistic mettle &
unequivocal medieval rage."

Fluorescent lights flicked on
once they heard the sword
clanging against cement
and the manager entered
wiping sweat from his head
and apologizing profusely.
He wore a navy polo shirt
with the company logo
as did the chagrined trainer
who was attempting to lure
the monster back inside
its chain-linked enclosure
by offering it a rank knot
of chickens tied to a pole.
It mostly just seemed tired.

Brian climbed unsteadily
into the unmarked Ford van
they used as an ambulance
and Paul held a washcloth
to the puncture wound
in his neck with one hand
but he had a beer in the other
and already he and Steve
were beginning to laugh

about how half-assed it was
and the manager promised
that next time would be
better, that a new one was
en route from Arkansas
and still mostly feral, so
next time they might see
what it felt like to be alive.

The Two of Us

I am an obscure semi-human from the hinterlands
as well as a nondescript songbird and an old shoe. I am
me not you. I am a god in one small valley of the Andes,
where I use my mind to make it rain. Which I just did
here in this poem, a small cloudburst to settle the dust
and raise good smells from the earth as the sun returns.

There is no limit to what I can do with these words
but the words themselves. For instance, I have recently
been yearning for a word to capture the feeling one
might get listening to a piano sonata when the sound
of the distant sirens outside begins to rise and fall
through the surface of the music like a lonely dolphin.

It is a word that would capture the threat of the outside
world leaking into a dimly lit interior full of beautiful
hunger. I'd like a word for that. Or at least its residue.
Maybe you feel the same, now that you're me not you.

Almost Invisible

You are there and you
are not there. Or here.

*

You are not anywhere
but you are reading THIS
and so you are somewhere.

*

Adverbs are inadequate.

*

When you are invisible
can you feel the wind
blowing through you?

Does your rib cage
feel like a ladder?

*

When you are invisible
can we gather round

to watch the quiet fire
of your thoughts?

*

And what happens when
you eat a sandwich?

*

And how about
when you spit?

*

And what happens when
you swallow aspirin?

Tiny twin moons?

*

How did this happen?

*

How did you learn
to give yourself
away so utterly

that you no longer
have hands to hold
what is not there?

The Light

I have been entered
said the man
and showed me his hand
slit clean as a cut
at the butcher.

That's quite an opening
I said
and slipped one
finger in.

It was pink
and unexpectedly cool.

What blade
did this?
I asked.

It was the light
he said.
It has always been

the light.

The Plot

Who knows, really?

For every day I move through summer air
easy as smoke

there is another where I am weighted
with mild despair

as if the sacks of gravel stooping my shoulders
were real.

I may well be moving
within the memory of another,

employed as an extra
in his recurring dreams.

I want to be a bone
in the body of something

larger. An animal
snuffling and panting

as they drag it from the woods,
strips of muscle tensing beautifully

even as its limbs
tear at the ropes.

Acknowledgments

32 Poems: "Nowhere"

American Poetry Review: "At Night," "The Cellar,"
   "The Subterranean Room"

Beloit Poetry Journal: "In the Himalayas," "The Monster"

Boston Review: "They Held It in Their Hands"

Brazenhead Review: "On the One Hand"

Copper Nickel: "Lazarus"

Forklift, Ohio: "Moles"

Iowa Review: "The Fact," "The Plot"

The Journal: "The City"

Nashville Review: "Island"

New Ohio Review: "The Meat of It"

No Tokens: "For the Person I Have Not Met"

The Offing: "Gag"

The Pedestal: "Sunflowers"

Pleiades: "Confessions"

Poetry Northwest: "Early November," "Ithaca," "The Phone Call"

Poetry U.S.A.: "Okay"

Revolver: "The Matrons," "There Are Things We Cannot See"

Salamander: "The Man with No Mouth"

Sixth Finch: "The Unnerving Thing"

The Sun: "Nobody Fails at Meditation"

Tahoma Review: "The Fable of the Man"

Thrush Poetry Review: "Rain"

Virginia Quarterly Review: "In the Book"

West Branch: "I Went to the Market"

Yemassee: "The Central Registry"

Leslie Bazzett

MICHAEL BAZZETT is the author of *You Must Remember This*, which received the 2014 Lindquist & Vennum Prize for Poetry; *Our Lands Are Not So Different*; and a chapbook, *The Imaginary City*. His poems have appeared in numerous publications, including *Ploughshares*, *The Sun*, *Massachusetts Review*, *Pleiades*, and *Best New Poets*. A longtime faculty member at The Blake School, Bazzett has received the Bechtel Prize from Teachers & Writers Collaborative and is a 2017 National Endowment for the Arts Fellow. He lives in Minneapolis.

milkweed
editions

Founded as a nonprofit organization in 1980, Milkweed
Editions is an independent publisher. Our mission is
to identify, nurture and publish transformative literature,
and build an engaged community around it.

milkweed.org

Interior design and typesetting by Mary Austin Speaker
Typeset in Fournier

Fournier is a typeface created by the Monotype Corporation
in 1924, based on types cut in the mid-eighteenth century by
Pierre-Simon Fournier, a French typographer. The specific cuts
used as a reference for Fournier are referred to as "St Augustin
Ordinaire" in Fournier's influential *Manuel Typographique*,
published in 1764 in Paris.